City of the Sun

Books by Stanley Nelson

The Brooklyn Book of the Dead
The Travels of Ben Sira
Driftin On a Nightriff
Idlewild
Immigrant (Volumes 1-4)
The Unknowable Light of the Alien
101 Fragments of a Prayer
Synesthetics/Edges of Sound (with Harry Smith)
*Pre-Socratic Points & Other New Poems**
*Limbos For Amplified Harpsichord**

* Available from Presa Press

City of the Sun

poems by
Stanley Nelson

PRESA :S: PRESS
Rockford, Michigan

ACKNOWLEDGMENTS

This project was supported by a grant from The Smith/The Generalist Association, Inc.

FIRST EDITION

PRINTED IN THE UNITED STATES OF AMERICA

ISBN: 978-0-9800081-2-8

Library of Congress Control Number: 2008923702

Exclusive European distribution through Gazelle Book Service Ltd.
White Cross Mills, Hightown, Lancaster, LA1 4XS, United Kingdom
sales@gazellebooks.co.uk www.gazellebooks.co.uk

US orders may be made directly to the publisher or to any reputable book wholesaler. (Baker & Taylor, The Book House, Coutts Information Services, Midwest Library Services)

Cataloging Information: 1. Nelson, Stanley, 1933 - ;
2. Contemporary American Poetry

PRESA :S: PRESS
PO Box 792 Rockford, Michigan 49341
presapress@aol.com www.presapress.com

Contents

City of the Sun

City of the Sun

1)
Here
in the City
of the Sun
clouds
dome
in preventive non

chalance

2)
Crickets ride
the backs of squirrels;

aardvarks
roil in anthills;

wolverines
claw at jaguars
unafraid
of the stripéd
beasts

3)
Here

City

4)
of the Sun

5)
megalopolis
becomes

heliopolis

6)
Fountains spout chorus girls;
rivers ruin the dry land;

buffaloes snort at jaguars
unafraid of the stripéd
                                        beasts

7)
          beasts

jaguars snarl at cheetahs;
unafraid

                              of the spotted

                                                                        beasts

8)
of the City of

Sun

9)
of the City of

10)
Sun

11)
Dome/e
ish
non

chalance

12)
Dominican friars
Become louts and liars;
Expatriate musicians
Become Black Magicians;
hypnotists become
litigious;
marlins snap at sharks
unafraid
of the saw-toothed

beasts

13)
Beasts

14)
beasts

15)
Here

16)
At the center of the Earth,
At its very core,
There is an insidious pulling
(or attraction) as Sun
Penetrates to the very last ism
Of the core of Earth
And Earth opens and rises up
To receive the penetration.
And the other stars
Go twinkling on
Yearning for the Earth
But receiving
Only the darkness of space
Icicle sparks of

Eternity

17)

At center of the Temple
Of the City of the Sun

Rises a proud pillar
Of herbs and precious gems.

Solarians
Contemplate

Rays of Sun
And chant

Pythagorean hymns
And sonnets

White flamingoes
And parrots

Bustle and hustle in underbrush

18)

lobsters become hoopsters;
klansmen become bagmen;
camels pursue rhinos
unafraid of the hornéd
beasts

19)
Beasts

20)
Beasts

21)
Ofofofofofofof

22)
City of Sun

23)
mobsters become lobsters;
bands become glands;
cocks become socks;
Bobcats paw at wolves

Unafraid

Of the grinnish

Beasts.

24)
Marmosets ride the backs of dolphins;
Geese play tag with coots;
Mimics play chess with bellhops;

Weasels poke at tigers

Unafraid

Of the fearsome

beasts

25)

A perpetual
Spotlight
Penetrates

To the very recesses
Of the City of the Sun
Ferreting out

Imitation magic workers
And ersatz Nostradami
And false John Dees

(whose magic shows
With Edward Kelly
Mediumized Elizabethans)

26)

Boasters become toasters;
Hipsters become dipsos;
Journals become urinals;
Lemurs pout at pit bulls

Unafraid

Of the slathering

Beasts

Beasts

27)
The High Priest
In the City of the Sun
Enters the Temple

At that hour
'Twixt dawn and night
When sun

Penetrates earth
With oscillation
And vibration

From the inner
And outer Cosmos
All life blinks

And stirs
In these vibrations
Swamps

Come alive
With all manner

Of beasts and birds:

Marshen and grackle
Redwing and clapper
Heron and plover

Gartersnake, copperhead.

28)
O
fofofofofofof

29)
City of Sun

30)
Mobsters become lobsters;
lawyers become foyers;
hustlers become rustlers;
hyenas snarl at panthers unafraid
of the black-sheened

beasts

31)
Beasts

32)

The paneled walls of the Temple
depict great scientists such as Kepler
and Einstein; great poets such as
Homer and Milton; great warriors
such as Hannibal and Napoleon; great
biblical heroines such as Ruth
and Miriam; great pagan heroines
such as Andromache and Clytemnestra;
great doctors such as Salk and Sabin;
great lawyers such as Clarence Darrow
and C. Vernon Mason; great actors such as
Olivier and Evans; great actresses such as
Garbo and Dietrich; great pilots such as Howard
Hughes and Ethan Russo; great businessmen such
as Howard Hughes and Henry Ford; great tennismen
such as John McEnroe and Jimmy Connors;
great tennisgals such as Serena and Venus Williams;
great catchers such as Yogi Berra and Johnny Bench;
great mobsters such as Meyer Lansky and Bugsy Siegal;
great opera stars such as Luciano Pavarotti and Maria
Callas; great bassists such as Charles Mingus and Percy
Heath; great quarterbacks such as Otto Graham and
Johnny
Unitas; great pulling guards such as Fuzzy Thurston and
Jerry Kramer; great playwrights such as Sophocles and
Arthur Miller; great journalists such as Maureen Dowd
and
Thomas Friedman; great sportswriters such as Red Smith
and Jimmy Cannon; great sportscasters such as Red
Barber
and Al Michaels; great saxmen such as Charlie Parker
and

Lester Young; great trumpeters such as Satch and Diz;
great flautists such as Jean Pierre Rampal and James
Galway; great middleweights such as Sugar Ray
Robinson
and Tony Zale; great sirens such as Dorothy Lamour
and Ava Gardner; great admirals such as Lord Nelson
and Hyman Rickover (father of the atomic submarine);
great Indian givers such as George Bush and Henry
Kissinger;
great comics such as Milton Berle and Henny
Youngman;
great strippers such as Gypsy Rose Lee and Sally Rand...

33)
A young and beautiful man
with a lute
met a country maid on a country road
outside the City of the Sun.
And the man with the lute
played for the country maid
madrigals of white wheat;
Apollo with a bow and quiver;
stirring airs and lullabies;
and the man with the lute
played madrigals
of white-bosomed maids
with golden marmosets;
white whippets in racing pose...

34)
the inner side

of the first wall
(the one next to the temple)
are shown all sorts
of mathematical figures
greater than those composed
by Euclid or Archimedes;
also are shown Watteau figures
bouncing spongeballs
playing hide and seek,
racing kites along the strand...

35)
Strand...

36)
On the outer walls of the Temple
are depicted processionals
with bells and gongs;
belted Franciscans;
marionettes with huge bulging eyes;
huge frogs with spectacles;
two-legged mules
with silver vests;
tuning forks with stubby toes;
Solarians bearing curative minerals:
chimeras with wings of salt
and lips of bronze;
Salty Peanuts decked out
in tux and tophat;
football analysts with ticker tape
in their pockets;

dinosaurs
twirling hula hoops
Mexican
with large sombreros
and slitlike eyes;
terrorists in bikinis;
druggists
wearing mason aprons;
masons wearing housewife
aprons;
curlers
bearing wheelbarrows
of rocks;
playmates mating;
knights
in Bermuda shorts;
damsels
with knobby breasts;
derelicts
with gold money clasps;
dentists
shackled to newscasters;
Watteau figures
bouncing spongeballs
skipping rope,
flying kites along the strand...

37)

At the core
of the earth
at its very

I AM
the earth
    breathes

in rhythm to
the cosmos
and fragments
of all planets

of the cosmos
coalesce
in its

breath
and the cosmos
breathes too

in rhythm
to Itself

CITY

38)
Munsters become slicksters;
Bands become glands;
Cocks become socks;
Bobcats paw at wolves

Unafraid

Of the grinnish

Beasts.

39)
Here
Of

40)
City

41)
Solarians
With softest breasts
(there are no women

In the City of the Sun)

Loll at their ease
(like Whitman)
In robes of color

Of rose petals
Observing the singular
Nature (like Thoreau)

Of the gingko tree.

42)
CITY

43)
the earth
breathes

44)
and in its breath
mingles with
breath of the

Sun
And in this
Joining

Is healing
And solace
And philosophy.

45)
dome/ish
breath of clouds
pre
ven tive non

chalance

46)
Solace O

Passages of o

47)
In the halls
Of the temple
Round the proud
Pillar
Of herbs and gems

Solarians
With huge
Erections

Wander in a trance
And pose as statues
Play at statues like
Little children
And they pose
As paper kites
And paper plates
And paper masks
And paper paper
And paper masks
And paper paper
And paper pumpkins
And paper shoes
And paper socks
(with holes in them)
And paper butterflies
And paper beetles
And paper Pomeranians
And paper tabbies
And paper McGavities
And paper hollyhocks
And paper cough drops

And paper...

48)
O inner beatitude;
The earth breathes...

49)
breathes:

50)
Breathes: and in this breathing
The Sun receives its breath in its penetration...

51)
And the Sun...

52)
...in its Infinite Beatitude

53)
Beatitude

54)
O blessed
O fervent
O holy-making

Solarians

To dance
With uplifted
Palms and faces

In the paths
And groves
And temples

Of the City of the Sun

55)
In the very depths of the Sun
In its very womb
It yearns for the moisture
Of earth, its waterfalls
And watersheds
Its lakes, seas,
And rivers:
And this reverberation
Affects the earth
And makes it gush
Like the source of rivers;
Always it is virgin for the Sun
Lifting to its demarcation,
Vibration, concentration
Concatenation of the Cosmos
Demonstration of the

Universe.

56)

Solarians
With softest
Breasts

(there are no females
In the City of the Sun)

Loll like Whitman
In soft robes
The color of rose petals

And regard Nature
(like Thoreau):
The Borax tree

Whose leaves fan out
Into little Tselichev
Faces

And whose leaves
Turn multihued
Every Leap Year;

The Zoloft butterfly
Who flits from
Gasoline can

To septic tank
Seeking caterpillars
To devour;

The ketchup beetle
Whose probing silicons
Groove on Big Mac wrappers;

The vellum hog
Who farts and belches
In beauty salons...
And many fearsome

Beasts.

57)
Beasts

58)
Zoloft Bor

Ax Prozac

We have seen, in the City of the Sun, how numbers become talismans...

We have known, in the City of the Sun, how magic workers bring down the power of the gods into their idols...

We have heard, in the City of the Sun, music beyond the spheres, like echoes of a Universal Organ...

59)

At noon
At the sun's very
Height

Solarians
Fill the riverbanks
And meadows; the
Earth opens like a moist
Pomegranate

Bursting into seed
And moistness
Awaiting Sun's frontal
Approach

60)

In the City
Of the Sun
When moon

61)

comes up

and mingles
its cool

fragrance
with the planets

Solarians

Peek out
From huts

And slowly
Slowly
Emerge

Into paths
And groves
Touching

Touching
Each other's
Soft soft

Breasts
Sucking
Each other's

Nipples
And then
They bow

In unison
And square dance
Round

The multihued
Fountain
And masturbate

To Sibelius
While chorus girls

Spout champagne
Grope
Their breasts

And cunts

62)

Si
        Belius

63)

Here

64)

City

65)

Sun

66)

Here
In the City of the Sun
Magic workers
Ward
Ward
Ward off
The planetary demons
With menses

And upraised
Middle
Fingers
Spreading
Capes with stars
Over lawn and grove
Warding
Ward
Ing

Al
Ways
Warding

67)
Ward!

68)
Ward off! Get

69)
thee gone!

70)
In the City of the Sun
All Solarians have fun;

Playing cops and robbers
And for apples bobbers;

Pinning tails on donkeys
Making do as monkeys;

Playing jacks and pinball
Pulling wire on schoolyard walls

71)
As has been said:
At noon in the City of the Sun
At its very
Height

Earth bursts
With seed and moisture
Overflowing
The very order

Of the Cosmos
And the Solarians
Stand in the pathways

With sly grins
And upraised hands
Chanting, chanting chanting:

o wise, o pretty
o sweet, o witty

O grand
Grant us solace
Become our whole
Burnt offering

Lead us to the magic
Spring of Consolation
Where the Itchy Ones

Live and thurl
All the while
With Thomas Stearns Eliot!

72)
The paths
Of the City
Of the Sun

Are strewn with roses
And tulips
Of every hue

And texture. Malamutes
And doves
Accompany Solarians

With empty cans
Of carnation milk
As acolytes

Play gongs
And kazoos
And strew

Crepe paper and
Ticker tape
Along the flower

Beds. Sumo wrestlers skip
With purple-
Tongued clowns
And grunt and fuddle

Fraudulently.

73)
Groves
Of the City
Are filled

With every manner
Of fruit tree:
Quince and persimmon

Plum, pear, pomegranate
But also the exotic
Jipjapa

Whose tendrils
Extend forty feet
And wondrous

Malamaba
Which sprouts
Fruit flies

Once a year
On January 3rd
Then descends

Into annual decline;

The skimp bush
Which sprouts
Beagle faces

April 1st and June 30th

74)
Of of

Of

Of

75)
It has been witnessed
And recorded:

In the City
Of the Sun
When moon

Comes up
And mingles
Its cool

Fragrance
With the planets

Solarians
Peek out
From huts

And slowly
Slowly
Emerge

Into paths
And groves
And then they bow

In unison
And square dance
Round

The multihued
Fountain
And masturbate

(not to Sibelius)
To Tchaikovsky

76)

The Way to Philosophize

The world's the book where the eternal Sense
Wrote his own thoughts
The living temple where,
Painting his very self with figures fair
He filled the whole circumference

Here then should each man read, and gazing find
        Both how to live and govern, and beware
Of godlessness; and, seeing God allwhere
        Be bold to grasp the Universal Mind.
But we tied down to books and temples dead
        Copied with countless errors from the life,
        These nobler than that school sublime we call.
O may our senseless souls at length be led
        To truth by pain, grief, anguish, trouble, strife...
          Turn we to read the one original...[1]

Joyfulness

Blissfulness

Peacefulness

Holiness

Giddiness

Artfulness

Boldfulness

Copelessness

Developness

Equalness

Forfendness

Gollyness

Harmlessness

Inwardness

Joyfulness

Loveliness

Miraculous

Nothingness

Originless

City

[1] Tomaso Campenella, as quoted in *Giordan Bruno and the Hermrtic Tradition*, Francis A. Yates, University of Chicago Press.

Fragrances

Fragrances

1.

Notwithstanding
An aroma of arches
Fragrance of tottering rain—
So dawn comes out

In pattering folds
As a courtesan peeking
From her boudoir. Arches
Reflect a domain
Of doves and nighthawks

Seen only by the initiate
The one who knows
The biding

The fountains, as if traced
By the mouth of a dying god.

2.

The dying god
Still sings of doves and nighthawks
Forming his mouth into a perfect O.

He knows the glint
Of the arches as the initiate
Knows the tottering rain
And the courtesan

Knows the scent of her boudoir.
But the aroma of arches
Must be aligned with the drizzling sun
Or the god will die in vain.

3.

The fountain projects
In the tottering rain

With panache, reflecting
Not just the arches
But also the *aroma*
Of the arches

As the courtesan
Prepares her boudoir.
Here the god is silent,
Preparing for his death

As the initiate
Prepares the doves
And nighthawks.

4.

The tottering rain
Like the fountain, reflects
Shadows of telephone lines

As the dying god,
His mouth an agony of silence,
Plunges downward
With shy giraffes
In a swoon
Of noon fantasia
And the doves
And nighthawks
Swerve with swallows
Along the sheltering arches.

5.

Notwithstanding
The initiate
Peers through the monochrome of rain

As dawn folds itself
Among the shadow
Of the arches

And seeks the dying god
Who must remain silent
In his dying agony

The initiate already
Swoons into noon fantasia
Like a crumbling
Shadow of the arches.

6.

The courtesan
In her boudoir
Cannot mimic

The scent of swerving rain
Or the presence of shy giraffes;
Now the arches

Reflect a pattering
Of pine and fir
As doves seek the rising sun
And nighthawks
Find the sheltering
Shadow of the arches.

7.

After storybooks and shy giraffes
The initiate consorts
With terns and gulls

Under the sheltering arches
Reflecting now a mélange
Of pine and fir.
Out of the deep shadows

Elegiac sunlight reflects
The throbbing throat,
The dying god.

8.

Mouth of the dying god
Frames silence on his lips
As the courtesan prepares her boudoir

With scents and illusions.
Emerging from dawn with shafts
Of sunlight, flocks of birds
Overwhelm the arches

In a fantasia yearning toward noon
Shielding the initiate
From coils of tottering rain.

9.

Notwithstanding
A song of eclipse
Deep deep in his heart
The initiate can't

Give voice to this song,
This prayer of eclipse;

To give it voice
Would doom the dying god
To a realm of harsh gongs,
Dissonant bassoons.

10.

The dying god
Caught in the shadow of the arches
Dreams instead of a realm
Of storybooks and shy giraffes,

Jugglers and magicians,
Disinherited knights,
Lutists with song
Already on their lips,

Bosomy courtesans
Décolletage with golden
Marmosets at the cleavage

Preachers in frock coats,
Assonant oboes and flugelhorns.

11.

In the agony of his dying
The god with song
Silent on his lips

Now forming the perfect O
Of solitude in his dying
A medley of sousaphones
Resonates with flute and piccolo

Reaching the deep deep heart
Of the initiate
And his song of eclipse.

12.

Notwithstanding
The song of eclipse
Must be framed before the pulse

Of noon fantasia
Overwhelms the white arches
Scattering the birds

As the courtesan
Open her boudoir
To the initiate with talismans,
And scents and illusions.

13.

The courtesan prepares her boudoir
Before the slow light of day
Pierces her scents

And illusions. She puts on
Her satin gown and watches
As flocks of birds
Presage early dawn

On the white arches.
Today she will receive no one
But the initiate and his deep song
Of eclipse.

14.

In the agony of his dying
The god tracing
Silence on his lips

Now forming the perfect O
Of solitude.
In his dying
A mélange of sousaphones
Resonates with flute and piccolo

Reaching the deep deep heart
Of the initiate
And his song of eclipse.

15.

Notwithstanding
The song of eclipse
Must be framed
Before the pulse

Of noon fantasia
Overtakes the white arches
Scattering the birds

As the courtesan
Opens her boudoir
To the initiate with talismans,
And scents and illusions.

16.

Pieces of noon fantasia
Pierce the chest of the dying god.
The eager lips
Yearn for the deep pulse of the initiate.

But his mouth collapses
Into its perfect O

Devoid of song of eclipse.
Stands of pine and fir
Behind the white arches
Harbor the various birds
And small furry beasts.

17.

Suddenly white arches
Are overwhelmed by flocks
Of falcons, signaling
A new song in the heart
Of the initiate, who kisses
The mouth of the dying god
Bringing his new song

To darkest places.
The courtesan applies secret scents,
Eagerly awaiting the initiate.

18.

Suddenly the plaza fountains
Flash into rigid sunlight,
A burst of noon fantasia

Illumining the fir and pine,
The breath of birds and small
Beasts. The initiate notices the mouth of the
dying god

Cannot form its perfect O,
The lips sagging into nondescript contagion,
The cheeks sucked in with weariness.

19.

The courtesan opens her boudoir
To the initiate as the god
Writhes in unbearable agony.

High above the arches
In the stark shadow
Of pine and fir
Falcons swerve and swallows
Dip down
Toward the plaza fountains.
The god's mouth sucks inward.
The god is dead.

20.

As the god dies, the initiate
Enters the courtesan's boudoir
Enticed by scents and talismans

And illusions. Suddenly
The white arches turn dark
Engulfed

By the shadow of pine and fir
And the shifting flocks of birds
Circling the plaza fountain
He makes love to her

Slowly, adoringly.
Afterwards, they lie
In each other's arms for a long time.

Then solemnly, adoringly,
She traces on his lips
The song of the dying god.

Genesis Vibes

Genesis Vibes

By the bitumen pits of Sodom
I lay down and wept
hearing the great salt dredge
of moonscape. Lot,

newly widowed, walks among
the salt statues
searching
for the lineaments
of her face. Hobbled Cain
wanders the deadest place
on earth, keening
keening for his murdered
brother. Ishmael
howls from the wilderness, progenitor

of a mighty nation, and Esau
prowls Sinai with four hundred men
seeking the brother

who betrayed him

By the burning bitumen pits of Sodom
In the shadow of the great
salt mines
under a new Moon
Noah dreams

of the Ark he will build
of the creatures he will save
of the daughters
who will give him
wine and seduce him. In the wilderness,
Hagar's son, progenitor
of a mighty nation
sports with Isaac. Jacob,
fearing Esau's wrath,
seeks pasture and herds
for a peace offering

in this most waste of places. Abraham,
asleep on a stone,

dreams of Yahweh's trials, Mesopotamian nights.

Along the great salt arc of Sodom
I lay with Moon
worshiping Moabites
circumcised for the rape of Dinah,
Jacob's only daughter,

and felt the sharp stone knife
pierce my foreskin,

as Simeon and Levi,
most fearsome of the brothers,
slew each indisposed
Moabite.

Dinah, avenged,
now dances in moonlight.

Simeon and Levi seek new spoils

searching moonscape

for jebuzite, hittite, hivite
japhethite, caananite, hamite

Bedouins
on donkeys
ride the moonscape

as Tubal-Cain descendant
of the first murderer on earth

forges iron implements
by the bitumen pits
while his father Lamech

screams that he is seventy fold
the murderer that was Cain
for killing a young boy
who merely wounded him.

Esau

Falls on Jacob's neck
and weeps
 in front of four hundred men.

Cain wails from his mask,
as Ishmael, progenitor
of a great nation,
 begs his father's forgiveness

and Isaac plays in the moonlight
musing on the journeys ahead.

Whirl
 Wind
 out of Cha

 os Yahweh
 thunders in his divination

dividing
the moon and stars

from the sun, Sky
from Sea. Abraham, stunned,
Shivers
before the Moongod. Cain

raises the stone knife
as Adam herds
the loping goats

and Esau
hunts the antelope and cheetah. Ishmael,
in moonlight, dreams
of his own

mighty nation. Abraham,
in homage, smashes
his chaldean idols

and begs for Sodom and Gomorrah.

But Yahweh looks back
On Gomorrah's flames, Sodom's
Desolation.

Sarah
skulks in her tent
bemused and rueful

of the child
she will deliver
in her old age. Rebecca

twirls pottery
on the moonscape and Rachel
smears chaldean idols

with her menses. Abraham
rides camels
with Bedouins
exultant
for the son of his old age. But Isaac
sees Jacob

emerging from Rebecca's womb

with his hand grasping
Esau's heel, sees already
the stone knife

dripping the blood
of circumcision, of sacrifice,

repentance.

Under the great salt drums of Sodom
I lay down and wept
yearning yearning

for the moon-piercing voice
of Yahweh. Reeling
Lot
stumbles across moonscape
chilled by the terrible wrath. Lascivious

Eve,

uncontainable, entices snakes

between her thighs

while her husband
covers himself in shame. At last
It comes, echoing

from desert stars and moonrays
at the edge of thornbushes
across the forbidding
hostile desert
and I yearn

for the great I AM, but hear
only a tearing of sounds
like thunder smashing stone.

Waste

land

of the deadest

place

on earth

scarp of pain and burning and strife, peopled
with jebuzite, hittite, moabite, ammonite
Here Yah
weh lurks in the night-heaven, waiting

to accept his role
above the other
moongods. But only

one man - Abraham from Ur of Chaldee -
heeds Yah
weh's appeal. Abraham
from Ur of Chaldee, feeling his
soul stir in the breath
of the Invisible God,

smashes the idols
turns his back
on graven images

to make his long journey
to a strange promised land.

Yahweh's
Ramshorn
pierces the dark
stillness
like nails of a crucifix. Rages
the heavens (angels congregate) roars
from mountaintop
and forest, makes

the ocean skip and dance,
twirls desert
sand dunes. Somber

Abraham
packs the mules
for the journey to Moriah
to sacrifice
Sarah's only son. Caravan

of Bedouins

passes over moonscape carrying

a rare treasure: Joseph
of the many-colored coat
abandoned Joseph who will soon become

Vizier of mighty Egypt.

In the lunar sands
Of a desert night

I lay down and wept

Yearning yearning

For the voice of Yahweh
The great I AM
But I heard

Only the boulders
Like a small lachrimating

Voice

Bringing distance

And graves

Wind

From deserted caves
Bringing dust and the debris

Of centuries

Voices
Of Adam and Eve

Weeping their wordspaces

Motion

Of Moabite, Hurrian, Jebuzite, Hittite

The desert caravan

Moving across lunar sands

Like a caravan

Of centuries

Joseph

Of the many-colored coat

Slowly slowly

Moves in a desert caravan

Toward black Egypt

Land of darkness and pain.

On moonscape

Yahweh as Elohim

Moves on the Face of the

Deep

His Shofar thunders

From the depths

To where angels

Applaud and move

Their wings in unison

On moonscape

Hagar protects Ishmael
From the wolves

            Lot falls on the neck of Cain
            And weeps and weeps
Searching for his wife
Among the salt

                        Pillars
Cain rebuffs Lot

                        Bitter for Yahweh's mark
Noah prowls the Ark
Counting each animal

                        Over and over
                        As his daughters make their plans
To ply him with wine
                        And seduce him
Abraham rides wild mules
                        With Bedouins

Sarah laughs for the child

She bore in her old age

While Isaac

Searches for the flint and kindling

For Sacrifice

Isaac

Searches for the flint

And kindling

While Yah

Weh

Proclaims

He is chief;

The Awesome One: among

The moongods

Walking in the cool of the evening

Proclaims by His fiery sword

And cherubim

Whose mouths form a perfect O
While Adam and Eve
Huddle in some desert cave
With their figleaves
(Eve in the waters
Milk of her nipples
Swirls and tipples
The evening tide)
Recollects Eve
Before the Serpent
When the stars aligned for her beauty
Joseph
Tells his brothers
Of his dream:
That he is chief among them

On moonscapes

Cain prowls the scarp

Esau the Red

Returning from the hunt
Beats his chest

For his lost birthright

Dinah, now avenged,

Dances in moonlight

Stibium-breathed with

Enticing limbs.

Jacob toils

Seven long years

For Laban

For the hand of Rachel

Then discovers he has gone in unto

Cowlike

Leah

And must tend Laban's pastures

And flocks

Seven more years

For Rachel - then goes in unto

Rachel seven times. Isaac

Trods the road to Moriah

In silence. What does he know?

What does he think?

Esau begs for the birthright

But blind Isaac is adamant.

On moonscape

Hagar shields her son from the fierce
wind

As Cain and Lot

Ride wild asses

With the Ludim, the Amonim, the Lebanim,

The Nephatilm.

Lamech and Tubal-Cain

Ride wild camels

On moonscape

With the Naphtuhim, Pathrusim, the Cathlusim and
Caophtorim

(ancestors of the Philistines)

Esau, Cain and Lot wander
In a trance
Among the salt pillars
Embracing them lasciviously. Leah
And her concubine drop one brother
After another
While Rachel remains barren and bitter
Finally, with immense birth pangs, she brings forth Joseph.

Jealous of Jacob's attention
And the many-colored coat

The brothers rip the coat off Joseph
And fling him into a bitumen pit
Where he is found by Moabites

On a caravan to Egypt
Jacob, lying on a stone in the desert,

Is visited by a strange creature -
Perhaps an angel -
Who wrestles him all night
And wounds his thigh
And tells him he will
Now be called Israel
And will be the progenitor
Of a mighty nation
That will change the world

Yah

Weh,
Wandering the Face of the Deep
Knows he is chief among the moongods
From the heavens
Roaring His mighty Shofar

Joseph is sold by Moabites
To Potiphar, Pharaoh's
                                        Chief steward. But Potiphar's
Wife
            Lusts after Joseph. Disrobes him. Thrown
            Into prison, Joseph interprets
The dreams of the baker and cupbearer.

And the cupbearer is slain, while the baker lives.

Joseph is brought to Pharaoh
And correctly interprets his dreams -

                        Seven lean years,
                        Seven fat year.

Tamar, dressing herself
As harlot, sleeps with Judah,
                                    Her father.

Then joins Hagar and Ishmael

On moonscape. Returning

From the hunt,
Famished Esau
Begs Jacob for lentils. But Jacob
Demands the birthright.

Pharaoh names Joseph
Vizier of all the land. Reuben
Rends his clothes
As expiation for his sin
Against Joseph.
Famine
Brings the brothers
To Egypt without Benjamin.

Joseph
Insists they return with Rachel's
Youngest son. They return with Benjamin
And Jacob. Yah

Weh's angels, invisible,
Sit and flutter their wings

By Jacob's tent. Pharaoh

Gives Jacob and his clan
The land of Goshen for pasture

And flocks and Jacob's progeny
Become numerous as the sands of the desert

Serpent hisses and slithers

Round Eve's heels
Enticing her to new ecstasies

While Yah
Weh's angels
Flitter and flutter
Through the Nightsky

By the bitumen pits of Sodom
I lay down and wept
Hearing the great salt dredge
Of moonscape.

And at last
Here here
In this deadest place on earth
I heard the great I AM
Like a desert tidal wave
Smashing from the Deep
Shattering stars and galaxies. And I saw

The long bondage
In Egypt (bricks without straw)
Emergence of a great leader
To take them out of bondage
The rainbow and the pillar of fire
The long migration through the desert
To a promised land

The broken clay tablets

And the golden calf

Moses beating the rock

For water

Smelt

The char

Of the Burning Bush

Still caught

In the trauma of His Perpetual Fire

Heidegger/HEIDEGGER

Heidegger/HEIDEGGER

1.

Being Console

Caring

Consoling

Dwelling Dwelling

Open

A Space Venture

Ing

Inward

Where Heart

Only

Knows

2.

Ripen O

Ripen

Ing Vine of the Heart

Way

In which you accept

Only this Way

3.

Open

Ripen

In your own

Accord

4.

Promise

Presence in Peace

To reside in Peace fourfold Presencing

5.

Earth

Sky

Gods

Mortals

6.

Snow

Vespers

7.

Con

Cealment

Un

Concealing

8.

Thing

Being

Con

Ceal

Being

Con
Cealing

9.

Presencing in Peace

To be brought to Peace sparing presencing

To remain in Peace fourfold presencing

10.

Snow

Vespers

Silence

Of a winter"s night

11.

Con

Cealment

Un

Concealing

12.

Thing

Ness

Being

Con

Ceiling

Being

In Un

Concealedness

13.

Mortals

Gods

Sky

Bridge

Waters

Care

Presence Un

Concealedness

14.

Care

Steeples

Vespers

Snow

15.

Un

Covering the

Con

Cealment Un

Concealedness

16.

Way

Without halt

Authentic

Origin

Growing into

Being

Authentic

The presencing Un

Conceals

17.

Winter

Snows

Home

Table

18.

Look to Sky

Look to gods

A Space

Presencing

A Life

To Dwell

19.

Un
Grund
Where Nothing

Ness

Dwells

20.

Between

Earth and Sky

Care a

Dwelling

Uncon

Cealedness

21.

From Being

Comes a Call

Care in

Dwelling

22.

Presenc

Ing

Care the

Call

Gods

Sky

Home

In Care

Ful Care

23.

Call to presencing

To inward Care

Un

Conceals

The sparse places

As in unfolding

Of manifold into one

Space

24.

Snow

Vespers

Table

Bed

Home

25.

Throwed

Ness to be thrown into a world

But Care brings us the Ungrund

Of Nothingness

26.

Thing

Ness

Of Sensation

Solace

In familiar things

Jug

Spoon

Chair

Bed

27.

Mediation

Between Thing

Ness

And Care

Brings us to the eternal

Indwelling

28.

Hard thugs

Accost us

On the Way—brick

Boulder, Thorn, Bough, Stone

29.

Opening

The Space

For Language, the

Poem

To bring us

Solace when the night-things—bat,

Nighthawk, owl—emerge.

30.

To be

Authentically

What you are

Encountering

Winter, snow, hootowl, vespers.

31.

Stand forth

On the Way

To Unconceal

edness

In the presencing

Of Care, always

In

dwelling

32.

Spatial

Locations

Bring us Art

Of Care,

Indwelling Care that ripens

Our hearts

Like clusters on the vine

33.

In the night

A stillness dwells

More solitary

Than steeple bells

And there is naught but peace

In the remotest fells

More peace and caring

Than angels tell.

34.

Average non-

Being

Countersalient

Countervalent

In worldly

Things

In

Terpretation of all

Entities

We encounter

In average

Doing-day

Ness

35.

Interpretable

But hidden in Darkness

Interpretation

As of footprints

Or finger

Prints

Access but always

Seek

Ing

Unconcealedness

Book

Shingle

Swamp

36.

Articulation

Of entities and enigmas

Bring release

But never

Consolation, Care

37.

Darkness veiling

Our Thing

Ness our ownmost

Day-to-day-ness?

38.

Average non

Being as
Countervailing
Countervalent

In everyday

Things

In

Terpretation of all

Entities

We encounter in average

Doing-day

Ness

39.

Interpenetrative

But hidden in Darkness

Interpretation

As of footprints

Or finger

Prints

Access but always

Concealed always

Seek

Ing Unconcealedness

In Being-there

Being-in-the world

40.

Boots

Books

Shingle

Swamp

41.

Articulation

Of entities and enigmas

Bring release

But never

Consolation, Care

42.

Darkness veiling

Our Thing

Ness our ownmost

Day-to-Dayness

43.

Ships

Shores

Coasts

Breezes

Birds

Lily

44.

Inward

Grace

Ges

Ture

Jests

Ingrown

The grace

The Just the

Bless

The just sorta

Blessed

45.

Thing

Ness

Overcomes

Our ownmost

Gesture toward

Toward

Being-in-the-world

46.

Lips cusps lisps

Cups

Fill Space

47.

Voice

Of the venture

Of the edges

Of sound

That is all that is worth

Doing

Out of the longing

Of the lyric sound of all

We could ever feel this

Groove

Of nuclei, nucleoli, quark

48.

Entities

On the Way

To Being

Enigmas
Veiled but Unconcealed

In Being-qua Being

49.

Seeking

Transparency

Inquiring

Ever

Seeking

But sanctify

The consoling

Stillness

50.

Access

To the hidden, the
Concealed

Is ours

In our ownmost

Being

51.

Ripening

Sound

In the very Spaces

Of your Being

Lyric

Sound

Stuns

Our Being-in-the-World

Supple

The just said

Stuns

52.

Opening

A World

With the justsaid

Stuns us

Into Being

Where we Ripen

Into

Ourselves

53.

Inward

The grace

The justsoit

Blesses

The soil

Of Being-in-the-World

54.

Chair

Broom

Totebag

Pen

55.

Entities

Obscure

The Transparent

Block

The grace

Fullness

Of Being

56.

Seeking

A ground

In Itself, escape

From

Entities

57.

Origins

Entities

Accost us

In the soundcore

That bedevils

Our dreams

58.

In

Dwelling

The Way

The ven

Ture

Care of our Being

There

59.

Desk

Drawer

Shelf

mat

60.

Care

Core

Dwell

Be

61.

Twas winter, and the Night

Was still, except the flutter

Of birdwings, and there was peace

More peace than man can utter

In his lifetime. So the poem

Ends, here on the quiet

Hillside, while Vespers

Call the pilgrim home.

About The Author

Stanley Nelson, *b.* 1933, is the author of 17 published books of poetry, most recently *Limbos For Amplified Harpsichord* (Presa Press, 2007) . He is best known for his long narrative poems, *Idlewild, The Brooklyn Book of the Dead, The Travels of Ben Sira* & the four-volume *Immigrant.* He is the recipient of the Thomas Wolfe Poetry Award. His work has appeared in over 50 publications & several anthologies, most recently *Inside The Outside - An Anthology Of Avant-Garde American Poets* (Roseanne Ritzema, editor, Presa Press, 2006). He has been the editor of *The Scene*, an anthology of plays from Off-Off Broadway. *The Unknowable Light of the Alien*, one of his many works of fiction, received a Small Press Book of the Year Award from *Library Journal.* Over 100 productions of his plays have been performed throughout the country & in England, & his play, *Poe: From His Life And Mind*, was cited in Best Plays of 1971 & given a national college tour by the New York Touring Company. He is a graduate of the University of Vermont. He is a native of, & continues to live in Brooklyn, New York.

www.presapress.com

Louis E. Bourgeois
Alice, $6.00
Kirby Congdon
God Is Dead (again), $20.00
Selected Poems & Prose Poems, $15.00
Hugh Fox
Time & Other Poems, $6.00
Blood Cocoon - Selected Poems of Connie Fox, $15.00
Eric Greinke
Selected Poems 1972-2005, $20.00
The Drunken Boat & Other Poems From
The French Of Arthur Rimbaud, $15.95
Wild Strawberries, $15.00
Kerry Shawn Keys
The Burning Mirror, $14.95
Richard Kostelanetz
PO/EMS, $6.00
Ronnie M. Lane
Morpheus Rising, $6.00
Linda Lerner
Living In Dangerous Times, $6.00
Lyn Lifshin
In Mirrors, $15.00
Glenna Luschei
Seedpods, $6.00
Total Immersion, $15.00
Stanley Nelson
Pre-Socratic Points & Other New Poems, $15.00
Limbos For Amplified Harpsichord, $17.95
City Of The Sun, $16.95
Roseanne Ritzema, (Editor)
Inside The Outside - An Anthology of
Avant-Garde American Poets, $29.95
Lynne Savitt
The Deployment Of Love In Pineapple Twilight, $6.00
Harry Smith & Eric Greinke
Up North, $6.00
Ben Tibbs
Poems, $6.00
Lloyd Van Brunt
Delirium, $6.00
Leslie H. Whitten Jr.
The Rebel - Poems by Charles Baudelaire, $7.50
A.D. Winans
This Land Is Not My Land, $6.00.
The Other Side of Broadway - Selected Poems, $18.00